FOOD LOVERS

QUICK & EASY

RECIPES SELECTED BY ALEKSANDRA MALYSKA AND JONNIE LÉGER

Trans
Atlantic
Press

All recipes serve four people, unless otherwise indicated.

For best results when cooking the recipes in this book, buy fresh ingredients and follow the instructions carefully. Make sure that everything is properly cooked through before serving, particularly any meat and shellfish, and note that as a general rule vulnerable groups such as the very young, elderly people, pregnant women, convalescents and anyone suffering from an illness should avoid dishes that contain raw or lightly cooked eggs.

For all recipes, quantities are given in standard U.S. cups and imperial measures, followed by the metric equivalent. Follow one set or the other, but not a mixture of both because conversions may not be exact. Standard spoon and cup measurements are level and are based on the following:

1 tsp. = 5 ml, 1 tbsp. = 15 ml, 1 cup = 250 ml / 8 fl oz.

Note that Australian standard tablespoons are 20 ml, so Australian readers should use 3 tsp. in place of 1 tbsp. when measuring small quantities.

The electric oven temperatures in this book are given for conventional ovens with top and bottom heat. When using a fan oven, the temperature should be decreased by about 20–40ºF / 10–20ºC – check the oven manufacturer's instruction book for further guidance. The cooking times given should be used as an approximate guideline only.

CONTENTS

TOMATO AND BREAD SKEWERS
ON PARMA HAM

Ingredients

3–4 thick slices white bread, cut into 1 inch (3 cm) cubes

2 cloves garlic

About ¼ cup / 50 ml olive oil

16 cherry tomatoes

2 sprigs thyme, leaves

6–8 small gherkins

8 slices Parma ham

2 tbsp. extra virgin olive oil

1 tbsp. lemon juice

Salt & coarsely milled pepper

Wooden skewers

Method

Prep and cook time: 15 min

1 Purée the garlic finely with the oil and briefly toss the bread cubes in the flavored oil. Preheat the broiler (grill).

2 Thread the tomatoes on wooden skewers with the bread, alternating tomatoes with bread. Sprinkle with thyme.

3 Cook on all sides under a hot broiler (grill) for about 5 minutes.

4 Drain the gherkins, slice lengthways and put on plates with the Parma ham. Mix the oil with the lemon juice and sprinkle over the gherkins and ham. Arrange the skewers on top and season lightly with pepper and salt. Serve at once.

PORK CHOPS
WITH MUSHROOMS

Ingredients

1–2 tbsp all-purpose (plain) flour

4 boneless pork chops

2 tbsp vegetable oil

For the mushroom sauce:

2 tbsp butter

1 (10-oz) package / 300 g button
mushrooms, quartered

1 onion, finely chopped

1 tbsp all-purpose (plain) flour

Scant 1 cup / 200 ml light cream

Salt and freshly ground pepper, to taste

2 tbsp coarse-grained French mustard

1-2 tablespoons milk, as needed

For the vegetables:

Scant cup / 200 ml vegetable broth
(stock)

1 lb / 400 g carrots, peeled and cut
into matchstick-size pieces

1 cup / 100 g sugar snap peas,
trimmed and halved

Method

Prep and cook time: 25 min

1 Spread the flour on a plate. Coat the chops with
the flour, shaking off the excess. Heat the oil in a
skillet, add the chops and cook until browned and
just cooked in the center. Remove from heat and set
aside, keeping warm.

2 To prepare the sauce, heat the butter in a skillet;
add mushrooms and onion and sauté until soft.
Sprinkle with the flour and sauté for 1 minute. Pour
in the cream, stirring constantly, and bring to a boil.
Season to taste with salt, pepper and mustard. Add
milk as needed to thin the sauce. Place the pork
chops in the sauce and keep warm over low heat.

3 Meanwhile, bring the vegetable broth (stock) to
a boil in a saucepan; add the carrots and simmer,
covered, for about 5 minutes. Add the sugar snap
peas and simmer 1 minute; drain.

4 Place the pork chops onto plates, spooning
mushroom sauce over the top. Serve with the
vegetables.

STIR-FRIED VEGETABLES WITH GINGER

Ingredients

2 tbsp oil

1 shallot, chopped

1 tbsp minced garlic

2 tsp minced fresh ginger root

1 tsp salt

2 medium carrots, peeled and chopped into bite-size pieces

½ lb / 200 g asparagus, trimmed and cut into bite-size pieces

½ cup water

½ lb / 200 g bok choy, chopped into bite-size pieces

½ lb / 200 g Napa cabbage (Chinese leaves), chopped

1¼ cups / 200 g broccoli florets

2 tsp sugar

1 tbsp rice wine

1–2 tbsp light soy sauce

2 tsp sesame oil

Method

Prep and cook time: 20 min

1 Heat the oil in a wok and stir-fry the shallot, garlic, ginger and salt for about 1 minute. Add the carrots and asparagus and stir-fry for about 30 seconds. Add the water and cook over high heat for about 2 minutes.

2 Add the bok choy, cabbage, broccoli and sugar; stir in the rice wine and soy sauce. Continue cooking for a further 3 minutes, stirring constantly. Drizzle the sesame oil over the top, divide into bowls and serve immediately.

LINGUINE WITH SALMON AND CHEESE-CHIVE SAUCE

Ingredients

14 oz / 400 g linguine

2 tbsp butter, divided

1 onion, finely diced

2 cloves garlic, minced

Scant ½ cup / 100 ml dry white wine

½ cup / 125 ml vegetable broth (stock)

1¼ cups / 150 g grated Gruyère cheese

2/3 cup / 150 g crème fraîche

Salt & freshly ground pepper, to taste

1 hot red chili pepper

1 lb / 450 g salmon fillet, skinned and cut into bite-size chunks

3 tbsp lemon juice

2 tbsp snipped chives

Method
Prep and cook time: 30 min

1 Cook the pasta in boiling salted water until al dente; drain and keep warm.

2 Meanwhile prepare the sauce: heat 1 tablespoon of the butter in a skillet; add onion and garlic and sauté until soft. Add the wine and broth (stock), then stir in the cheese and crème fraîche and simmer for about 5 minutes. Season with salt and pepper and set aside, keeping warm.

3 Wearing gloves to prevent irritation, seed and devein the chili and slice into thin strips. Heat the remaining butter in a skillet and fry the salmon and chili for 2–3 minutes. Season with salt, pepper and lemon juice.

4 Stir the chives into the sauce, toss with the drained pasta and arrange on plates, topped with the salmon.

FRIED NOODLES WITH SHRIMP

Ingredients

14 oz / 400 g noodles

3 tbsp. sesame oil

1¾ cups / 200 g sugar snap peas, trimmed

1 red bell pepper, halved, cored and cut into strips

2 cloves garlic, peeled and finely chopped

1 tbsp. sesame seeds

1 chili, deseeded and finely chopped

1 cup / 200 g broccoli florets

2 scallions (spring onions), cut into rings

14 oz / 400 g shrimp (prawns), peeled and deveined

Fish sauce

Method

Prep and cook time: 30 min

1 Cook the noodles in boiling, salted water until al dente, then drain, refresh in cold water and drain well. Keep warm.

2 Heat the oil and sauté the sugar snap peas, bell pepper, garlic, sesame seeds and chili. Then add the rest of the vegetables and stir-fry for 3–4 minutes. Add the noodles and shrimp and stir-fry for a further 2–3 minutes, until all the ingredients are cooked but still have a little bite. Season well with fish sauce and serve.

CHICKEN NOODLE SOUP

Ingredients

10 oz / 300 g chicken breast, cut into bite-size pieces

1 tbsp. cornstarch (cornflour)

2 tbsp. sesame oil

1 clove garlic, peeled and finely chopped

½ inch / 1 cm piece ginger, peeled and finely chopped

1 tsp. curcuma (turmeric)

4 cups / 1 liter vegetable broth (stock)

1 stick lemongrass, cut into strips

7 oz / 200 g rice noodles

4 scallions (spring onions), cut into rings

1 small Napa cabbage (Chinese leaves), chopped

8 cherry tomatoes, quartered

2 tomatoes, diced

4 tbsp. light soy sauce

4 tbsp. lime juice

Thai basil, to garnish

Method

Prep and cook time: 25 min

1 Mix the chicken pieces and the cornstarch (cornflour) in a bowl.

2 Heat the sesame oil in a saucepan and fry the chicken until lightly browned. Add the garlic, ginger, and curcuma (turmeric) and sauté, then pour in the vegetable broth (stock) and bring to a boil.

3 Add the lemongrass to the soup and simmer for about 5 minutes.

4 Put the rice noodles in the soup and simmer for a further 1–2 minutes over a low heat. Add the Napa cabbage (Chinese leaves), scallions (spring onions), cherry tomatoes, and tomatoes and warm thoroughly.

5 Season to taste with soy sauce and lime juice. Garnish with Thai basil and serve.

PENNE WITH POTATOES, CHICKEN AND GREEN BEANS

Ingredients

12 oz / 300 g small new potatoes

½ lb / 250 g green beans, trimmed and halved

2 small skinless boneless chicken breasts

Salt and freshly ground pepper, to taste

4 tbsp olive oil, divided

2½ cups / about 11 oz / 300 g penne

1 tbsp finely chopped fresh basil

1 tbsp finely chopped fresh parsley

About 1 oz / 40-60 g Parmesan cheese

Method

Prep and cook time: 35 min

1 Scrub the potatoes and boil them in a large pan of salted water until cooked. Meanwhile, bring a saucepan of salted water to boil and add the beans and cook until tender-crisp, 8-10 minutes. Drain in a colander under cold running water to stop the cooking; set aside.

2 Season the chicken breasts with salt and pepper. Fry in 1 tablespoon of the oil for about 5 minutes on each side until cooked through, then remove from the skillet. Slice diagonally into strips and keep warm.

3 Cook the penne in boiling salted water until al dente; drain.

4 Meanwhile, heat the remaining oil in a large skillet. Halve boiled potatoes and add them to the skillet along with the green beans and cook, stirring frequently. Season with salt and pepper. Combine with the penne and gently stir in the chicken strips, basil and parsley.

5 Arrange onto plates. Shave Parmesan cheese over the top and serve.

TOMATO SALAD
ON TOASTED BREAD

Ingredients

5 tbsp vegetable oil, divided

1 clove garlic, halved

4 large or 8 small baguette slices

2 tbsp balsamic vinegar

1 tbsp lemon juice

1 pinch sugar

1 good pinch dry mustard

Salt and freshly ground pepper, to taste

2 large tomatoes, sliced, halved or quartered according to size

½ cup / 100 g yellow tomatoes, halved

½ cup / 100 g red cherry tomatoes, halved

1 stalk celery, thinly sliced

1 red onion, thinly sliced

1 tbsp finely chopped scallion (spring onion) greens

½ cup / 80 g crumbled blue cheese (such as Gorgonzola) or sheep's cheese

Method

Prep and cook time: 20 min

1 Heat 3 tablespoons of the oil in a skillet and sauté the garlic 30 seconds. Remove from the skillet with a slotted spoon and discard. Return the skillet to the heat and fry the bread slices until golden; set aside.

2 In a large bowl, whisk the remaining oil with the vinegar, lemon juice, sugar and mustard, to make a vinaigrette; season with salt and pepper. Add the tomatoes, celery, onion and scallion (spring onion) greens and toss to coat with the dressing.

3 Pile the salad onto the fried bread slices and scatter the cheese over. Serve at once.

SALMON WITH HERBS AND LEMON

Ingredients

1 whole salmon fillet, with skin

Salt, to taste

1 lemon

Scant ¼ cup / 50 ml olive oil

1 small onion, finely chopped

½ bunch parsley, finely chopped

½ bunch basil, finely chopped

1/3 bunch dill, finely chopped

½ inch / 1-cm piece fresh ginger root, peeled and minced

1–2 cloves garlic, minced

Freshly ground pepper, to taste

1 tsp sea salt

Method

Prep and cook time: 25 min

1 Preheat the oven to 400°F (200°C / Gas Mark 6). Grease a long, shallow baking dish (large enough to hold the salmon in a single layer).

2 Lightly salt the salmon. Using a zester or vegetable peeler, zest the lemon and slice into thin slivers. Halve, then juice the lemon into a medium bowl. Add the oil, onion, parsley, basil, dill, ginger, garlic, lemon zest, and pepper.

3 Place the salmon in the baking dish and cover with the lemon-herb mixture. Season with the sea salt. Bake for about 15 minutes or until firm. Serve immediately.

STIR-FRIED CHICKEN WITH GINGER

Ingredients

1 lb / 500 g skinless boneless chicken breasts, sliced into strips

1 egg white

1 tbsp all-purpose (plain) flour

3 tbsp vegetable oil

2 scallions (spring onions), thinly sliced

1 tsp minced fresh ginger root

1 red bell pepper, diced

1 small hot chili pepper, deseeded and finely chopped

2 tbsp rice wine

1-2 tbsp soy sauce

1 tbsp black bean paste

Method
Prep and cook time: 30 min

1 Combine the chicken with the egg white in a medium bowl. Blend the flour to a smooth paste with 2 tablespoons water and mix with the chicken.

2 Heat the oil in a large skillet or wok and sauté the chicken until firm. Transfer to a plate and keep warm; return the wok to the heat.

3 Add the scallions (spring onions) and ginger; sauté lightly. Add the bell pepper, chili pepper, rice wine, soy sauce and bean paste; return the chicken to the wok and stir-fry for a few minutes, until cooked through. Season to taste and serve with rice.

KEDGEREE

Ingredients

2 tbsp vegetable oil

1 small onion, chopped

½ tsp garam masala*

1¼ cups / 300 g long-grain rice

2½ cups / 600 ml fish broth (stock)

½ bunch scallions (spring onions), chopped

12 oz / 300g smoked haddock, flaked

Salt and freshly ground pepper, to taste

¼ cup / ½ stick / 50 g butter, melted

2–3 hard boiled eggs, chopped

4 tbsp chopped fresh parsley

Lemon juice, to taste

Lemon wedges, to garnish

Method

Prep and cook time: 35 min

1 Heat the oil in a large skillet; add the onion and garam masala and sauté until the onion is translucent. Add the rice and continue to sauté for about 1 minute, until the rice grains are well coated.

2 Pour in the fish broth (stock) and bring to a boil; cover and simmer for about 20 minutes or until the rice has absorbed the liquid. Add the scallions (spring onions) and fish about 5 minutes before the end of cooking time. Season with salt and pepper.

3 Stir in the butter, chopped eggs and parsley; cook, stirring gently over medium heat for 1–2 minutes. Season to taste with lemon juice, garnish with a few lemon wedges and serve.

*Garam masala, a "warming" spice blend used in Indian cuisine, often contains black pepper, cinnamon, cloves, coriander, cumin, cardamom, fennel and other spices. Find it in Asian groceries and gourmet shops.

CHICKEN KEBABS WITH COUSCOUS

Ingredients

1½ cups / 250 g couscous

1 lb / 500 g skinless boneless chicken breasts, cut into wide strips

Salt & freshly ground pepper, to taste

Juice of 1 lemon, divided

1 small zucchini (courgette), finely diced

2 tomatoes, finely diced

1 (14-oz) can / 400 g chickpeas, rinsed and drained

1 bunch parsley, finely chopped

4 radicchio lettuce leaves

Lemon wedges, to garnish

Cherry tomatoes, to garnish

Method

Prep and cook time: 40 min

1 Soak 12 wooden skewers in enough water to cover them for 15 minutes (to prevent burning). Preheat the broiler (grill).

2 Cook the couscous according to the packet instructions.

3 Thread the chicken strips onto the skewers. Season with salt and pepper and sprinkle with lemon juice, reserving 2 tablespoons. Marinate for 10 minutes.

4 Broil (grill) the kebabs for about 10 minutes, turning once, until browned and cooked through.

5 Meanwhile, combine the zucchini (courgette), tomatoes, chickpeas and parsley with the couscous; season with salt, pepper and the reserved lemon juice.

6 Fill the radicchio leaves with the couscous salad and arrange on plates with the chicken kebabs and lemon wedges. Garnish with tomatoes.

CRAB SALAD BOATS

Ingredients

8 oz / about 200 g cooked crab meat, picked over to remove shells

1 shallot, finely chopped

2 tbsp mayonnaise

1 tbsp sour cream

Salt and cayenne pepper, to taste

12 large Belgian endive leaves

2 oz / 50 g pistachios, roughly chopped

2 plums, pitted and sliced into thin strips

Method

Prep and cook time: 20 min

1 Mix together the crab meat, shallot, mayonnaise, and sour cream in a bowl. Season with salt and cayenne pepper.

2 Place a spoonful of crab salad onto each endive leaf. Sprinkle each with chopped pistachios, then scatter a few slices of plum on top. Serve immediately.

ASIAN NOODLES WITH PORK

Ingredients

About 1 lb / 400 g Chinese noodles

2 oranges, preferably organic

1 tbsp vegetable oil

1¼ lb / 600 g pork loin, trimmed and cut into thin strips

Scant 1 lb / 400 g sugar snap peas, trimmed

1 orange bell pepper, cored and cut into thin strips

2 red chili peppers, chopped (wear gloves to prevent irritation)

8 scallions (spring onions), trimmed and chopped

½ pint / cherry tomatoes, halved

1 tbsp honey

Light soy sauce, to taste

Method

Prep and cook time: 25 min

1 Put the noodles into a bowl, pour boiling water over them and let stand for about 3 minutes, then drain.

2 Zest the oranges and reserve. Peel the oranges thoroughly and cut out the segments, avoiding the white pith and skin, but catching the juice.

3 Heat the oil in a wok, add the pork and stir-fry until browned. Transfer to a plate.

4 Return the wok to the heat and add the sugar snap peas and bell pepper. Stir-fry for about 3 minutes. Then add the chilies and stir in the reserved pork, the noodles, scallions (spring onions), cherry tomatoes and orange segments with the orange juice. Cook for a further 1–2 minutes to heat through. Add honey and soy sauce. Serve, sprinkled with orange zest.

CHICKEN SALAD
WITH BEET LEAVES

Ingredients

4 chicken breasts

Oil, for frying

Salt & freshly milled pepper

4 tbsp. olive oil

2 tbsp. cider vinegar

1 tbsp. coarse Dijon mustard

2 cups / 200 g lamb's lettuce

2 cups / 200 g beet (beetroot) leaves

1 yellow bell pepper, deseeded and cut into cubes

2 beefsteak tomatoes, cut into wedges

Method
Prep and cook time: 25 min

1 Cut the chicken into strips. Heat a little olive oil in a skillet and fry the chicken on all sides until cooked thoroughly. Season with salt and pepper and place on the side.

2 Make a vinaigrette dressing using the olive oil, cider vinegar, Dijon mustard, and salt and pepper. Place the lamb's lettuce, beet (beetroot) leaves, bell pepper, tomatoes and chicken in a bowl, pour in the vinaigrette dressing and toss. Season to taste with salt and pepper and serve.

PENNE WITH TOMATOES AND ASPARAGUS

Ingredients

3½ cups / 400 g penne

1 lb / 500 g green asparagus

4 tbsp. olive oil

1 clove garlic, peeled and finely chopped

1 pinch chili flakes

Scant ½ cup / 100 ml vegetable broth (stock)

1 lb / 500 g plum tomatoes

1 bunch / 75–100 g arugula (rocket)

Salt & freshly milled pepper

Method

Prep and cook time: 30 min

1 Cook the penne in boiling, salted water until al dente.

2 Peel the lower third of each asparagus spear and cut at an angle into pieces about 1 inch (3cm) long.

3 Heat the olive oil and sauté the asparagus with the garlic and chili flakes. Add the vegetable broth (stock), cover and cook for 3–4 minutes.

4 Quarter the tomatoes, removing the hard cores at the top. Add to the asparagus and cook for a further 4–5 minutes. The asparagus should still have a little bite, but the tomatoes should be beginning to collapse.

5 Drain the pasta and add to the vegetables along with the arugula (rocket). Toss to combine, reheat briefly and serve seasoned to taste with salt and pepper.

OMELETTE WRAPS WITH HAM

Ingredients

4 tbsp butter

8 eggs, beaten

½ lb / 250 g thinly sliced ham

Lettuce leaves, thinly sliced

2 medium carrots, peeled and cut into thin strips

Salt and freshly ground pepper, to taste

Method

Prep and cook time: 25 min

1 Heat 1 tablespoon of the butter in an 8-inch (20-cm) nonstick skillet and pour in quarter of the egg mixture, swirling to coat the pan. When the eggs have set, transfer the omelet to a plate and repeat with the remaining butter and eggs to make four omelettes.

2 Arrange the ham, lettuce and carrot strips over the omelettes; season with salt and pepper and roll up to form a wrap. Slice in half along the diagonal and serve.

SHRIMP RISOTTO

Ingredients

1½ tbsp butter

1 tbsp olive oil

1 lb / 500 g shrimp (or prawns), peeled and deveined

1 red onion, finely chopped

1 clove garlic, minced

Heaped 1 cup / 250 g Arborio rice

2/3 cup / 150 ml dry white wine

3 cups / about 750 ml vegetable broth (stock), hot

¾ cup / 100 g frozen fava beans (broad beans)

¾ cup / 100 g frozen peas

2 tbsp crème fraîche

Juice of 1 lime

2 tsp chopped fresh parsley

Salt and freshly ground pepper, to taste

Method

Prep and cook time: 40 min

1 Heat the butter and oil in a large pan; add the shrimp (prawns) and sauté until barely pink; transfer to a plate and set aside.

2 Add the onion and garlic to the pan and sauté for 1–2 minutes. Add the rice and stir until the grains are translucent, about 5 minutes. Stir in the wine and cook until it has evaporated. Then gradually add the hot broth (stock) ½ cup at a time, stirring and adding the next ½ cup when the last addition has been absorbed.

3 Add the beans and peas after about 10 minutes, and continue in this way until the rice is soft, 15–20 minutes.

4 Stir in the crème fraiche, lime juice, parsley and shrimp; season to taste with salt and pepper and serve.

SPAGHETTI WITH BACON, WALNUTS, AND GORGONZOLA

Ingredients

14 oz / 400 g spaghetti

2 tbsp. nut oil

1 onion, finely chopped

4 oz / 100 g diced bacon

2 tomatoes, deseeded and diced

½ cup / 50 g shelled walnuts

Some fresh parsley

Salt & freshly milled pepper

4 oz / 100 g Gorgonzola cheese

Method

Prep and cook time: 25 min

1 Cook the spaghetti in boiling, salted water until al dente, then refresh in cold water and drain.

2 Heat the oil and fry the onion and bacon until golden brown. Add the tomatoes and walnuts, fry briefly, then add the pasta and fry briefly. Shred the parsley leaves and add them to the pasta. Season with pepper and a little salt.

3 Crumble the Gorgonzola over the pasta and serve at once on plates or in bowls.

PORK CHOPS WITH APPLES

Ingredients

3 tbsp vegetable oil, divided

4 pork chops

½ tsp curry powder

½ tsp honey

Salt and freshly ground pepper, to taste

2 apples, quartered and cut into bite-size chunks

2 red onions, sliced

2 tbsp pine nuts

1 tbsp freshly chopped basil leaves, to garnish

Method
Prep and cook time: 25 min

1 Preheat the oven to 250°F (130°C/ Gas Mark ½).

2 Heat 1 tablespoon of the oil in a nonstick grill skillet and sauté the chops on both sides until brown. Transfer to a baking dish.

3 In a small bowl, mix the curry powder with the honey and 1-2 tablespoons water. Brush the meat with the mixture and season with salt and pepper. Bake in the oven for 15-20 minutes, until the meat is just cooked in the center.

4 Meanwhile, add the remaining oil to the skillet, then add the apples, onions and pine nuts and fry all together for 2–3 minutes. Season with salt and pepper.

5 Put the chops on warmed plates, add a little of the apple and onion to each and serve scattered with basil.

POTATO PANCAKES

Ingredients

2¼ lb / 1 kg boiling potatoes, peeled and grated

1 onion, finely grated

1 egg

Scant 1 cup / 100 g all-purpose (plain) flour

Salt and freshly ground pepper, to taste

Vegetable oil, for frying

Method

Prep and cook time: 30 min

1   Preheat the oven to a low setting. Line a baking sheet with several layers of paper towels.

2   Spread the grated potatoes and onion on a kitchen towel and roll up jelly-roll (swiss roll) style. Twist towel tightly to wring out as much liquid as possible.

3   Combine the grated potatoes and onion in a bowl. Carefully mix in the egg and flour. Season well with salt and pepper. With your hands, shape into 2-tablespoon mounds, flattening them to form pancakes.

4   Heat about 1 inch (2 cm) of oil in a skillet until hot; add a few pancakes at a time without crowding the pan. Cook on both sides, pressing flat with a spatula, until golden brown. Arrange on the baking sheet and place in the oven to keep warm; repeat with the remaining pancakes. Serve hot.

ZUCCHINI
WITH SPINACH, GOAT CHEESE, AND CHICKPEAS

Ingredients

4 tbsp. olive oil

1 tsp. dried thyme

2 cloves garlic, finely chopped

2 zucchini (courgettes), sliced thickly

3 cups / 300 g baby spinach

1 bunch mint

2 cups / 300 g can chickpeas, rinsed and drained

1 tbsp. capers

Juice of ½ lemon

Sea salt & freshly milled pepper

1½ cups / 200 g goat cheese

Method

Prep and cook time: 40 min

1 Mix the olive oil with the thyme and the garlic. Pour over the zucchini (courgettes) and marinate for about 20 minutes.

2 Remove the zucchini from the oil and place under the broiler (grill) for about 6–8 minutes. Season with salt and pepper.

3 Mix the zucchini with the spinach, mint, chickpeas and capers and pour the lemon juice and the marinating oil over them. Toss the salad.

4 Season with salt and pepper, sprinkle the crumbled goat cheese over the top, and serve.

Published by Transatlantic Press

First published in 2010

Transatlantic Press
38 Copthorne Road, Croxley Green, Hertfordshire WD3 4AQ

© Transatlantic Press

Images and Recipes by StockFood © The Food Image Agency

Recipes selected by Aleksandra Malyska and Jonnie Léger, StockFood

ISBN 978-1-908533-57-9

Printed in China